Mathematics Topical Problem Sums

Joseph D. Lee

2nd EDITION PRIMARY 3

EPB is an imprint of SNP Education Pte Ltd.

© 1998 SNP Publishing Pte Ltd
© **1999 SNP Education Pte Ltd**

Published by
SNP Education Pte Ltd
162 Bukit Merah Central #04-3545
Singapore 150162

First published 1998
Reprinted 1999, 2000, 2001

Illustrations © 1999 SNP Education Pte Ltd

First published in 1998 by SNP Publishing Pte Ltd

Cover design by Albert Tan
Illustrated by Heng Kock Ham

ISBN 9971 0 5870 7

Printed by South East Printing Pte Ltd

PREFACE

PRIMARY THREE MATHEMATICS TOPICAL PROBLEM SUMS
is written in accordance with the **latest Primary School Mathematics Reduced-Content Syllabus** currently used in all schools in Singapore.

The main objective of this book is to **help the pupil improve his problem solving skills**. To achieve this, a **systematic coverage of all topics** with their relevant exercises has been designed. The language used is also kept simple and clear.

This book incorporates the following features.

TOPICAL PROBLEMS

This book contains 9 units of **Topical Problems**. **Worked Examples** are included at the beginning of each unit, where the pupil is guided step by step towards solving the various types of problem sums. These are followed by **Practice Problems** where the pupil is tested on his ability to solve common problem sums based on the topic. More problem sums follow in **Challenging Problems**, which require more thinking skills and creative problem solving strategies.

REVISION PROBLEMS

3 units of **Revision Problems** are included to help the pupil revise and reinforce the skills acquired in the preceding topics.

ANSWER KEY

An answer key is provided at the end of the book for the pupil or his tutor to check his answer.

It is my hope that this book will help the pupil improve his problem-solving skills.

JOSEPH D. LEE

CONTENTS

TOPICAL PROBLEMS 1

ADDITION AND SUBTRACTION

WORKED EXAMPLE 1

Daniel and Sam have 897 bottle caps altogether. If Daniel has 358 bottle caps, how many more bottle caps does Sam have than Daniel?

358

Daniel

Sam

897

?

$$897 - 358 = 539$$

Sam has 539 bottle caps.

$$539 - 358 = 181$$

Sam has **181** more bottle caps than Daniel.

WORKED EXAMPLE 2

A farmer had 1 231 chickens. He sold away 443 chickens and 287 chicks were hatched. How many chickens were there on the farm in the end?

1 231

?   443

$$1\ 231 - 443 = 788$$

After 443 chickens were sold, there were 788 chickens left on the farm.

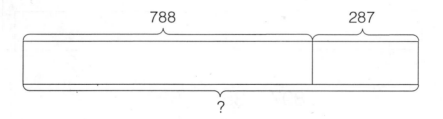

788   287

?

$$788 + 287 = 1\ 075$$

There were **1 075** chickens on the farm in the end.

WORKED EXAMPLE 3

James has 346 stickers. Paul has 177 more stickers than James and 78 more stickers than Roland. How many stickers do the three boys have altogether?

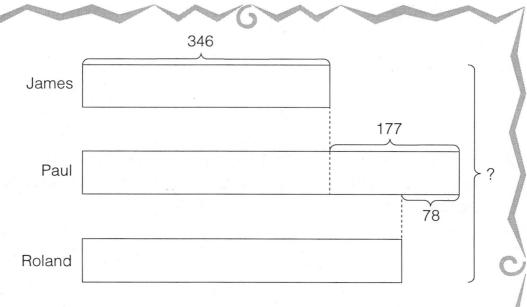

$$346 + 177 = 523$$

Paul has 523 stickers.

$$523 - 78 = 445$$

Roland has 445 stickers.

$$346 + 523 + 445 = 1\ 314$$

The three boys have **1 314** stickers altogether.

Read and then answer each question carefully. Show your working and statements clearly.

1. Mingde and Huihui have 1 293 stamps altogether. If Mingde has 868 stamps, how many more stamps does he have than Huihui?

2. A farmer collected 2 614 eggs, 3 019 eggs and 2 796 eggs in 3 different weeks. How many eggs did he collect altogether?

3. On a public holiday, 6 819 people visited the zoo. 2 912 of them were men and 1 355 were women. The rest were children. How many were children?

4. A book has 1 019 pages. Nancy read 423 pages last week and 376 pages this week. How many pages has she not read?

5. Paul has 2 147 stamps. 568 of them are Malaysian stamps, 335 are Hongkong stamps and the rest are Singapore stamps. How many Singapore stamps has he?

6. Mr Chen collected 3 142 oranges. 95 of them were bad and thrown away. If he sold away 1 896 oranges, how many oranges had he left?

7. Susan has 56 beads. Wendy has 17 beads more than Susan. Cindy has 24 beads less than Wendy. How many beads does Cindy have?

8. Sue has 87 stickers. Perry has 48 stickers less than Sue but 16 stickers more than Kevin. How many stickers does Kevin have?

9. A town had 7 211 people. Last year, 457 people moved out while 898 people moved in. Find the new number of people in the town.

10. A cinema has 1 210 seats. During the first show, there were 937 people seated. During the second show, 129 seats were not taken. What was the total number of people who watched the two shows?

11. Last week, 2 018 tourists came to Singapore by airplane, 875 tourists came by ship and 688 tourists came by train. How many tourists came to Singapore in all?

12. In November, 2 867 Chinese tourists and 4 987 Japanese tourists visited Singapore. Of these, 2 989 left Singapore by the end of November. How many of these tourists were left in Singapore after November?

Solve each of these problems, showing your working and statements clearly.

13. Junming and Xueli have 4 215 pictures altogether. If Junming has 549 pictures less than Xueli, how many pictures does Xueli have?

14. Mr Ahmad had 432 eggs. He ate 14 of them and broke 17. 33 of them hatched into chicks. How many eggs had he left?

15. Rick scored 2 416 points in a game. Mark scored 729 points less than Rick. How many points did they scored altogether?

16. Tom and Mike have 213 marbles altogether. Mike and Sam have 162 marbles altogether. If Sam has 94 marbles, how many marbles does Tom have?

17. 1 410 books were sold in March and April in all. 737 books were sold in March and 843 books were sold in May. How many books were sold in April and May altogether?

18. Mr Bai has 15 more blue pens than black ones. If he has 43 blue pens and 17 red pens, how many pens has he?

19. Jason and Bob have 193 marbles altogether. Bob has 47 marbles less than Jason. If Jason now gives 15 marbles to Bob, how many more marbles does Jason have than Bob?

20. Mingming has 26 bottlecaps more than Jiande. If Mingming has 41 bottlecaps, how many bottlecaps must he give to Jiande so that both will have the same number of bottlecaps?

21. Mingli and Shiyun have the same number of paper clips. When Mingli gives 16 paper clips to Shiyun, Shiyun has thrice as many paper clips as Mingli. How many paper clips does Shiyun have now?

$S + 16 = 3m$ $m = S - 16$

$16 + S = 3m$

$m = S$

22. After Ali had given 42 rubber bands to Simon, they had the same number of rubber bands. If they had 110 rubber bands altogether, how many rubber bands did Ali have at first?

23. Rizali had 21 hair clips more than pins. She gave away 13 pins and had 48 hair clips and pins left. How many hair pins had she left?

24. Julie had 43 more pencils than pens. When she gave away 17 pens, she had twice as many pencils as pens. How many pens and pencils had she altogether?

MULTIPLICATION AND DIVISION

WORKED EXAMPLE 1

483 oranges are put into 7 boxes equally. 23 oranges are taken away from one box. How many oranges are there left in that box?

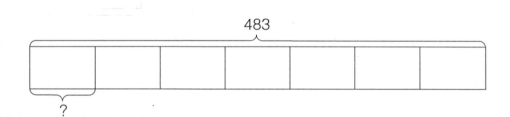

$$483 \div 7 = 69$$

There are 69 oranges in each box.

$$69 - 23 = 46$$

There are **46** oranges left in that box.

WORKED EXAMPLE 2

Mr Edmund has 8 boxes of 198 eggs each. He repacks all the eggs into 6 boxes equally. How many eggs does he pack into each box?

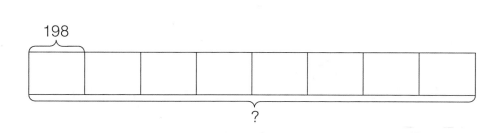

198

?

$8 \times 198 = 1\ 584$

There are 1 584 eggs altogether.

$1\ 584 \div 6 = 264$

He packs **264** eggs into each box.

WORKED EXAMPLE 3

Each boy has 4 balloons and each girl has 7 balloons. How many balloons do 12 boys and 9 girls have altogether?

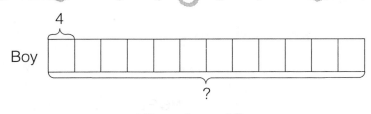

Boy

$12 \times 4 = 48$

The 12 boys have 48 balloons altogether.

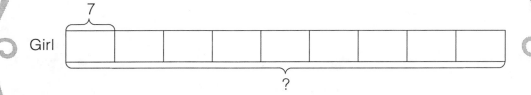

Girl

$9 \times 7 = 63$

The 9 girls have 63 balloons altogether.

$48 + 63 = 111$

12 boys and 9 girls have **111** balloons altogether.

Read and then answer each question carefully. Show your working and statements clearly.

1. 213 paper clips are shared equally among Sue, Jane and Alice. If Alice gives 24 paper clips to Sue, how many paper clips has Sue altogether?

2. Each packet had 234 sweets. Mrs Liang bought 3 packets and gave 87 sweets away. How many sweets had she left?

3. There were 4 packets of 18 mothballs each. They were collected and put into 3 boxes. How many mothballs were there in each box?

4. Tim, Bob and Jeffrey have 17, 36 and 49 marbles respectively. If they share all their marbles equally, how many marbles will each boy get?

5. Each box had 8 chocolates. Mrs Wu bought a dozen boxes and ate 29 chocolates. How many chocolates had she left?

6. Peter has 19 white balloons, 23 red balloons and 18 yellow balloons. He has half as many balloons as Peide. How many balloons has Peide?

7. Lisa had 216 pictures. She gave 28 pictures to each of her 3 cousins. How many pictures had she left?

8. Mrs Wang bought 6 dozen eggs and broke 9 eggs. How many eggs had she left?

9. Dick has 26 bottlecaps. Jack has thrice as many bottlecaps as Dick but half as many bottlecaps as Tom. How many bottlecaps does Tom have?

10. Chalk is sold in boxes of 35 pieces each. Mr Chen bought 5 boxes. If he already has 78 pieces of chalk, how many pieces of chalk has he altogether?

11. For every paper boat that Lina makes, Harry can make 2 paper boats. If they make 117 paper boats altogether, how many paper boats does Harry make?

12. Each box of 100 marbles has 37 blue marbles and 29 green marbles. The rest are yellow marbles. How many yellow marbles do 5 such boxes have?

Solve each of these problems, showing your working and statements clearly.

13. On Children's Day, a teacher gave 37 pupils 7 biscuits each. If she had 3 boxes of 100 biscuits each, how many biscuits had she left?

14. A class of pupils is divided into 7 teams. Each team has 6 pupils but one team has 1 pupil less. How many pupils are there in the class?

15. Janet, Nina and Julie bought 4 boxes of tissue paper and got 8 packets of tissue paper free. Each box of tissue paper had 16 packets of tissue paper. If they shared the tissue paper equally, how many packets did each girl get?

16. A ferry can carry 123 passengers while a ship can carry 415 passengers more. How many passengers can 1 ferry and 2 ships carry altogether?

17. Daniel and Gary scored 1 032 points in a game altogether. If Gary scored twice as many points as Daniel, how many points did Gary score?

18. After giving 16 coins to Jeremy, Sally had twice as many coins as Jeremy. If they had 144 coins altogether, how many coins did Sally have at first?

19. Mike and Paul have 87 coins altogether. If Mike has twice as many coins as Paul, how many coins does Mike have?

20. Liling had 24 clips more than Huixia. After she gave 5 clips to Huixia, Liling had twice as many clips as Huixia. How many clips did Liling have left?

21. Pingping has 41 coins less than Wenyi. If Pingping now has 13 coins more, she will have half as many coins as Wenyi. How many coins does Wenyi have?

22. Yuehua and Pingyi have 384 beads altogether. If Yuehua has twice as many beads as Pingyi, how many beads does Yuehua have?

23. Mrs Liu has thrice as many pears as apples. If she has 84 pears and apples altogether, how many pears does she have?

24. When 306 stamps are shared among Pat, Keqin and Rahim, Pat got twice as many stamps as Keqin and Rahim together. If Keqin got 18 stamps more than Rahim, how many stamps does Rahim get?

TOPICAL PROBLEMS 3

LENGTH

WORKED EXAMPLE 1

Mike is 1 m 54 cm tall. Bob is 17 cm taller than Mike but 9 cm shorter than Patrick. How tall is Patrick?

Mike | 1 m 54 cm

Bob | 17 cm

Patrick | 9 cm

?

1 m 54 cm + 17 cm + 9 cm = 1 m 80 cm

Patrick is **1 m 80 cm** tall.

WORKED EXAMPLE 2

Ribbon A is twice as long as ribbon B. Ribbon C is twice as long as ribbon A. The total length of ribbons A, B and C is 469 cm. Find the length of ribbon C.

Ribbon A

Ribbon B

Ribbon C

?

469 cm

2 + 1 + 4 = 7 units

7 units → 469 cm

1 unit → 469 ÷ 7 = 67 cm

4 units → 4 × 67 = 268 cm

The length of ribbon C is **268 cm**.

WORKED EXAMPLE 3

Rod P is 42 cm shorter than rod Q. Rod R is 17 cm shorter than rod Q. If the three rods have a total length of 154 cm, find the length of rod P.

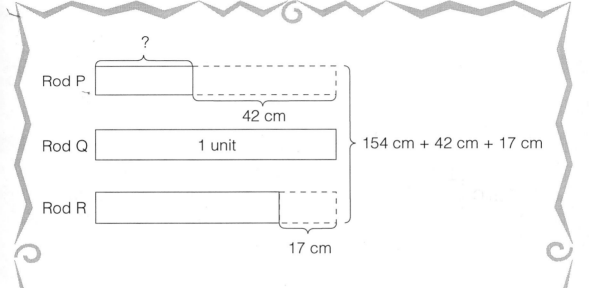

Rod P

?

Rod Q   1 unit   42 cm

Rod R   17 cm

154 cm + 42 cm + 17 cm

3 units → 154 + 42 + 17 = 213 cm

1 unit → 213 ÷ 3 = 71 cm

Length of rod P = 71 − 42 = 29 cm

The length of rod P is **29 cm**.

Read and then solve each question carefully. Show your working and statements clearly.

1. Susan had 15 m 9 cm of ribbon. She used 2 m 56 cm of the ribbon to wrap a present and 28 cm of it to tie her hair. Find the length of ribbon she had left.

2. The map shows Pam's house, an MRT station, a post office and a shopping centre. How much closer to Pam's house is the shopping centre than the post office?

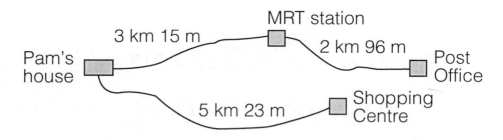

MRT station

3 km 15 m

Pam's house

2 km 96 m

Post Office

5 km 23 m

Shopping Centre

3. The total height of Paul and Jill is 3 m 26 cm. The total height of Jill and Sam is 3 m 11 cm. If Sam is 1 m 65 cm tall, how tall is Paul?

4. Jeremy is 1 m 72 cm tall. Brendan is 27 cm shorter than Jeremy and 15 cm shorter than Nick. Find Nick's height.

5. The total height of Alan and Bill is 3 m 12 cm. If Alan is 1 m 63 cm tall, how much taller is he than Bill?

6. The total length of strings A and B is 7 m 2 cm. String A is 2 m 28 cm shorter than string B. What is the length of string B?

7. Rod X is 4 m 61 cm long. It is 1 m 75 cm longer than rod Y and 2 m 55 cm shorter than rod Z. What is the total length of rods Y and Z?

8. Towns P and Q are 3 km 6 m apart. Towns Q and R were 2 km 91 m apart. Rachel drove from town P to town Q to town R, and then back to town Q. Find the total distance she drove.

9. A piece of ribbon was cut into three pieces. Their lengths were 4 m 19 cm, 1 m 77 cm and 2 m 44 cm. What was the length of the original piece of ribbon?

10. A farmer placed 10 poles at equal distances apart along a straight line. The distance between every two adjacent poles was 76 cm. Find the distance between the first and the last pole.

11. The distance between P and Q is thrice the distance between Q and R. Find the distance between P and R in metres and kilometres.

P   4 974 m   Q   R

Solve each of these problems, showing your working and statements clearly.

12. Mrs Liang had 3 pieces of cloth. They were 7 m 68 cm, 6 m 21 cm and 9 m 15 cm respectively. She used 3 m 79 cm of the largest piece of cloth to make a curtain and 2 m 46 cm of the shortest piece to make a dress. How much cloth had she left altogether?

13. A piece of yellow ribbon was twice as long as a piece of green ribbon. When 1 m 27 cm of the yellow ribbon was cut away, the piece of yellow ribbon was 2 m 25 cm longer than the piece of green ribbon. How long was the piece of yellow ribbon at first?

14. A black pole 3 m 21 cm long was 89 cm longer than a white pole. When part of the black pole was cut away, it was 1 m 3 cm shorter than the white pole. How much of the black pole was cut away?

15. Lucy is 1 m 58 cm tall and Mike is 1 m 74 cm tall. The total height of Lucy and Mike is equal to that of Sam and Pat. If Pat is 1 m 63 cm tall, how tall is Sam?

16. Ribbon A was twice as long as ribbon B. After 159 cm of ribbon A was cut away, ribbon A was half as long as ribbon B. Find the original total length of ribbons A and B.

17. Rope X is twice as long as rope Y. Rope Z is thrice as long as rope Y. The total length of the three pieces of rope is 516 cm. What is the length of rope X?

18. Towns A and B were 9 km 86 m apart. David started from town A towards town B while Rick started from town B towards town A. Some time later, David was 4 km 378 m away from town A and Rick was 3 km 485 m away from town B. How far apart were they?

19. String X is 34 cm longer than string Y. String Z is 58 cm longer than string Y. If the total length of strings X, Y and Z is 233 cm, find the total length of strings X and Z.

20. A piece of wire 358 cm long is bent to form a rectangle ABCD as shown. Find the length of BC.

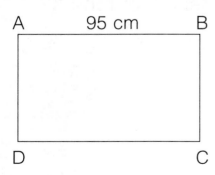

A   95 cm   B

D   C

WEIGHT

WORKED EXAMPLE 1

The total weight of a box of 42 apples is 6 kg 500 g. Each apple weighs 149 g. What is the weight of the box?

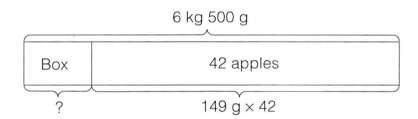

6 kg 500 g

Box	42 apples
?	149 g × 42

$$149 \times 42 = 6\ 258$$

The total weight of the 42 apples is 6 kg 258 g.

$$6 \text{ kg } 500 \text{ g} - 6 \text{ kg } 258 \text{ g} = 242 \text{ g}$$

The weight of the box is **242 g**.

WORKED EXAMPLE 2

There are three cakes, A, B and C. B weighs four times as much as A. A weighs twice as much as C. If B is 972 g heavier than A, how much heavier is B than C?

Cake A

972 g

Cake B

?

Cake C

8 – 2 = 6 units

6 units → 972 g

1 unit → 972 ÷ 6 = 162 g

8 – 1 = 7 units

7 units → 7 × 162 = 1 134 g

B is **1 134 g** heavier than C.

WORKED EXAMPLE 3

Andrew has 485 g of sugar, Jack has 117 g of sugar and David has 247 g of sugar. Find the total weight of sugar Andrew must give to Jack and David so that each boy has an equal weight of sugar.

485 g

Andrew

117 g

Jack

247 g

David

Total weight of sugar = 485 + 117 + 247
= 849 g

3 units → 849 g

1 unit → 849 ÷ 3 = 283 g

Total weight of sugar Andrew must give to Jack and David = 485 − 283 = 202 g

Andrew must give **202 g** of sugar to Jack and David.

Read and then answer each question carefully. Show your working and statements clearly.

1. Mrs Li bought 3 kg 120 g of fish, 1 kg 655 g of prawns and 4 kg 896 g of vegetables. What was the total weight of food she bought?

2. The total weight of Gary, Mark and Rohan is 180 kg 649 g. If Gary weighs 57 kg 258 g and Mark weighs 69 kg 966 g, how heavy is Rohan?

3. Jane poured 1 kg 876 g of green beans and 2 kg 555 g of red beans into an empty bottle. The total weight of the bottle of beans was 4 kg 696 g. Find the weight of the empty bottle.

4. A packet of sweets weighs 1 kg 60 g. A packet of flour weighs 344 g lighter than the packet of sweets but 188 g heavier than a packet of coffee powder. How much does the packet of coffee powder weigh?

5. A basket with 8 fishes weighs 958 g altogether. The basket weighs 182 g when empty. If each fish weighs the same, how heavy is each fish?

6. Peter and John have a total weight of 77 kg 450 g. Peter weighs 38 kg 690 g. How much lighter does he weigh than John?

7. Edwin weighs 41 kg 720 g. He is 4 kg 295 g heavier than Mark and 2 kg 880 g lighter than Sam. What is the total weight of the three boys?

8. An empty box weighs 138 g. 7 identical cans of fruit, each weighing 636 g, are put into the box. Find the total weight of the box of cans of fruit in kilograms and grams.

9. The total weight of 6 identical bags of flour is 870 g. What is the total weight of 10 such bags of flour?

10. Each book weighs 349 g and each photograph album weighs 512 g. Find the total weight of 4 books and 3 photograph albums in kilograms and grams.

11. Each large pizza weighs 326 g more than each regular pizza. If each large pizza weighs 821 g, how much do 6 regular pizzas weigh? Give your answer in kilograms and grams.

12. Two bags, X and Y, contain rice. Bag X weighs seven times as much as bag Y. The two bags weigh 2 192 g. How much heavier is bag X than bag Y?

Read and then answer each question carefully. Show your working and statements clearly.

13. Jianhui and Guoqiang weigh 108 kg altogether. If Jianhui is 4 kg lighter than Guoqiang, find Jianhui's weight.

14. The total weight of a bottle of milk and a packet of sweets is 1 kg 21 g. The total weight of a bottle of milk and a box of biscuits is 1 kg 347 g. If the box of biscuits weighs 525 g, how heavy is the packet of sweets?

15. A bag of sugar weighs as much as two 200 g weights, two 100 g weights and two 50 g weights. How heavy is the bag of sugar?

16. In the figure shown, what is the weight of X?

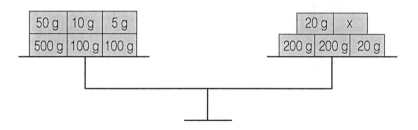

17. Parcel A weighs half as much as parcel B. Parcel B weighs four times as much as parcel C. The total weight of parcels A and C is 648 g. Find the weight of parcel B.

19. There are three fish tanks, A, B and C. B weighs six times as much as A and twice as much as C. If C weighs 36 kg more than A, find the total weight of A, B and C.

19. There are three pieces of rock, X, Y and Z. Y is 2 463 g heavier than X. Z is 1 914 g heavier than Y. The total weight of Y and Z is 8 628 g. How heavy is X?

20. Cindy has 267 g of beans, May has 132 g of beans and Ann has 444 g of beans. What is the total weight of beans Ann must give to Cindy and May so that each girl has the same weight of beans?

21. Each kilogram of grade A rice costs $5 and each kilogram of grade B rice costs $3. 2 kg of grade A rice are mixed with 2 kg of grade B rice to form grade C rice. How much does each kg of grade C rice cost?

Practice Problems

Read and then solve each question carefully. Show your working and statements clearly.

1. A farmer collected 7 213 eggs in a week. He sold 2 185 eggs on Tuesday and 2 866 eggs on Friday. How many eggs did he have left?

2. Raja has three books with 897 pages, 1 017 pages and 954 pages respectively. How many pages are there in the three books?

3. Chenghua has 1 485 Singapore stamps. He has 598 Malaysian stamps less than Singapore stamps. How many stamps does he have in all?

4. On a public holiday, 3 809 people visited the zoo. If 1 548 of them were children and the rest were adults, how many fewer children than adults were there?

5. Meiling and Wenhua have 141 coins altogether. Wenhua and Hanmin have 173 coins altogether. If Hanmin has 95 coins, how many coins does Meiling have?

MW 141
WH 173
H   95

MW   141
WH   173
H 95
? = M

6. Kevin has 72 blue marbles and 45 green marbles. If he has 24 fewer yellow marbles than blue marbles, how many marbles does he have?

7. Janet has 54 pins. Sue has 19 pins more than Janet but 6 pins less than Pam. How many pins does Pam have?

8. Qinqin has 33 beads less than Yinyin. If Qinqin has 48 beads, how many beads do they have altogether?

9. In a game, Junjie scored 688 points and Jianhui scored 115 points more than Junjie. How many points did they score altogether?

10. During a harvest, a farmer collected 1 854 papayas and 1 201 watermelons. If 207 of the fruits were bad, how many fruits were good?

11. John has 42 toy cars. He has twice as many toy cars as Mark. How many toy cars do they have in all?

12. Mark is 1 m 67 cm tall. Tom is 8 cm taller than Mark and 18 cm taller than Jane. How tall is Jane?

13. To reach town Y from town X, a man can take road A followed by road B or take road C. How much further must he travel if he takes road C?

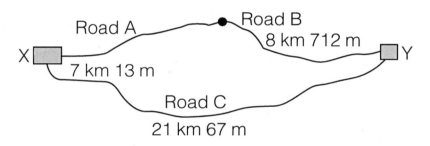

Road A

Road B
8 km 712 m

X

7 km 13 m

Road C
21 km 67 m

Y

14. Mrs Fang bought 9 m of cloth at $5 per metre. If she paid the cashier $50, how much change did she get?

15. A box with 8 cakes weighs 838 g. If each cake weighs 98 g, what is weight of the box?

16. Mrs Ma bought 4 kg of meat at $7 per kg and 7 kg of prawns at $9 per kg. How much money did she spend altogether?

17. Each bag of flour weighs 375 g and each bag of salt weighs 182 g. What is the total weight of 3 bags of flour and 4 bags of salt? Give your answer in kilograms and grams.

Solve each of these problems, showing your working and statements clearly.

18. Sam has 14 more toy cars than Peter. They have 62 toy cars altogether. If Sam now gives 5 toy cars to Peter, how many toy cars does Peter have?

19. Baoli has 24 hair clips more than Huifen. If Baoli has twice as many hair clips as Huifen, how many hair clips do they have altogether?

20. Rachel has 42 more pencils than Jane. Sandy has 23 fewer pencils than Jane. The three girls have 124 pencils altogether. How many pencils do Rachel and Sandy have in all?

21. Janet and Claire have the same number of beads. If Janet gives 12 beads to Claire, Claire will have thrice as many beads as Janet. How many beads do they have altogether?

22. Mark had 91 more marbles than Alvin. After Mark gave away 19 marbles, he had four times as many marbles as Alvin. How many marbles did Mark have at first?

23. Peter and Rose had 82 stickers altogether. After Peter gave 16 stickers to Rose, they had an equal number of stickers. How many stickers did Peter have at first?

24. Danny walked from A to B. At the same time, Victor walked from B to A. Some time later, Danny was 2 km 476 m away from B and Victor was 1 km 899 m away from A. If A and B were 5 km apart, how far apart were Danny and Victor?

A   B

25. Street lamps along a straight expressway are placed such that the distance apart between each adjacent pair of lamps is 120 m. Find the distance between the second and the seventh lamp.

26. A piece of red ribbon was 304 cm long. When 19 cm of it was cut away, it was thrice as long as a piece of green ribbon. How much longer was the red ribbon that the green ribbon at first?

27. The total weight of Getha, Paul and Jinyi is 157 kg 930 g. The total weight of Paul and Jinyi is 110 kg 690 g. If Paul weighs 57 kg 950 g, how much heavier is Jinyi than Getha?

28. 4 metal cubes and 3 wooden cubes weigh 3 650 g altogether. 9 metal cubes and 3 wooden cubes weigh 6 450 g altogether. How heavy is each metal cube?

29. In the diagram shown, the weighing scale will only be balanced if one 100 g weight is removed and seven 10 g weights are added. What is the weight of X?

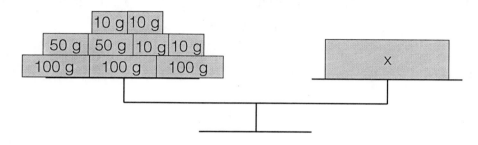

MONEY

WORKED EXAMPLE 1

> Melvin and Andy shared $14 equally. If Andy spent $2·35 on a pencil case, how much money did he have left?

$14

?

$$14 \div 2 = 7$$

Andy got $7.

$$7·00 - 2·35 = 4·65$$

Andy had **$4·65** left.

WORKED EXAMPLE 2

Peter and Sam have $31·05 altogether. If Sam has $14·60, how much more money does Peter have than Sam?

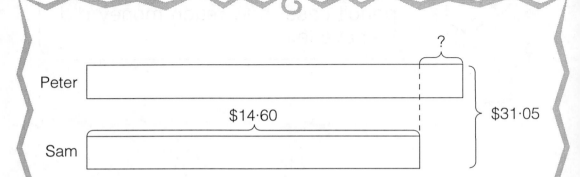

Peter

$14·60

Sam

?

$31·05

31·05 − 14·60 = 16·45

Peter has $16·45.

16·45 − 14·60 = 1·85

Peter has **$1·85** more than Sam.

Jim bought 7 pencils at 35¢ each. If he paid with a $5 note, how much change did he get?

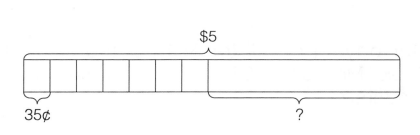

$5

35¢   ?

$7 \times 35¢ = 245¢$

The 7 pencils cost $2·45 altogether.

$5 - 2·45 = 2·55$

He got **$2·55** change.

Read and then solve each question carefully. Show your working and statements clearly.

1. Meimei has $17·60, Dehui has $14·55 and Qiqin has $29·85. How much money do they have altogether?

2. After buying a doll for $41·30 and a toy train for $23·90, Mr Qiu had $31·40 left. How much money had he at first?

3. Miss Ma had $81·20. She bought a clock and a bag and had $13·35 left. If she bought the clock for $32·75, how much did she pay for the bag?

4. Patrick has $57·60. Bob has $38·50 more than Patrick. How much money do they have altogether?

5. Meihua had $63·05. She spent $19·20 on Monday and $28·55 on Tuesday. How much money had she left?

6. Mr Fang's monthly income is $1 084. He spends $366 on food, $124 on transport and saves the rest. How much money does he save each month?

7. Mrs Wu bought 8 eggs at 15¢ each. If she paid with a $2 note, how much change did she get?

8. Rick has $100. If he buys 7 shirts at $12 each, how much money will he have left?

9. Alice had $43·15. After buying 6 files at $4 each, how much money had she left?

10. John had $30·80. He used $3·80 to buy a pen and the rest of the money to buy 9 identical book stands. How much did each book stand cost?

11. Sam had $71·40. He bought 8 identical books and had $23·40 left. How much did each book cost?

12. $81 is shared among Sue, Pat and Tom equally. If Sue gives $9·75 to Pat, how much money will Sue have left?

Solve each of these problems, showing your working and statements clearly.

13. Alvin has $8·85. John has $2·90 more than Alvin but $7·65 less than Mark. How much money does Mark have?

14. Fatimah and Kasim have $92 altogether. If Fatimah has $18 more than Kasim, how much money does Fatimah have?

15. Alan and Susan have $61·30 altogether. If Alan has $42·95 and he uses $27·45 to buy a shirt, how much less money will Alan have than Susan?

16. Dahua bought 7 exercise books and 4 rulers. Each exercise book cost 80¢ and each ruler cost half as much as each exercise book. How much money did he spend in all?

17. Roger has four times as much money as Edwin. If Roger has $120 more than Edwin, how much money do they have in all?

18. $60 is shared between 2 boys and 1 girl. If the girl gets twice the amount each boy gets, how much money does each boy get?

19. Nina has $14·15 and John has $23·85. How much money must John give to Nina so that both will have the same amount of money?

20. Jim and Dan have $24 altogether. If Jim gives $2 to Dan, he will have thrice as much money as Dan. How much money does Jim have?

21. Each towel costs $7 and each toothbrush costs $3. Mr Fu has $252. How many more toothbrushes than towels can he buy with the same amount of money?

22. A man bought 5 bottles of shampoo at $7 each. At a sale, each bottle of shampoo was sold at $5. How many more bottles of shampoo could he buy if he had bought the shampoo at the sale?

23. The table below shows the things which Mr Haniff bought for his new flat. How much money did he spend in all?

THINGS BOUGHT	AMOUNT
Sofa set	$863
Television set	$1 279
Radio set	$989
Dining table	$328

CAPACITY

WORKED EXAMPLE 1

> A bottle can hold 1 ℓ 42 ml of water. A jar can hold 1 ℓ 435 ml of water more. How much water can both containers hold in all?

1 ℓ 42ml

Bottle

1 ℓ 435 ml

Jar

?

1 ℓ 42 ml + 1 ℓ 435 ml = 2 ℓ 477 ml

The jar can hold 2 ℓ 477 ml of water.

1 ℓ 42 ml + 2 ℓ 477 ml = 3 ℓ 519 ml

Both containers can hold **3 ℓ 519 ml** of water in all.

WORKED EXAMPLE 2

A container has a capacity of 5 ℓ. 1 ℓ 338 ml of water and 2 ℓ 95 ml of water are added into the container, respectively. How much more water can the container hold?

5 ℓ

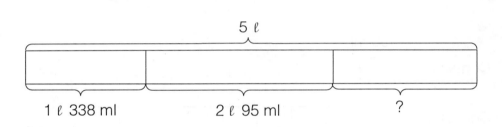

1 ℓ 338 ml   2 ℓ 95 ml   ?

1 ℓ 338 ml + 2 ℓ 95 ml = 3 ℓ 433 ml

3 ℓ 433 ml of water is added into the container altogether.

5 ℓ – 3 ℓ 433 ml = 1 ℓ 567 ml

The container can hold **1ℓ 567 ml** of water more.

WORKED EXAMPLE 3

Container A has 483 ml of water. Container B has nine times as much water as container A and 1 ℓ 212 ml of water less than container C. How much water is there in container C?

483 ml

Container A

Container B

1 ℓ 212 ml

Container C

?

Amount of water in container B = 9 × 483
= 4 347 ml

Amount of water in container C = 4 347 + 1 212
= 5 559 ml

There are **5 ℓ 559 ml** of water in container C.

Read and then answer each question carefully. Show your working and statements clearly.

1. There are three containers, X, Y and Z. X can hold 4 ℓ 24 ml of water. It can hold 1 ℓ 385 ml of water more than Y and 678 ml of water less than Z. Find the total capacity of Y and Z.

2. The capacity of a pail is 9 litres. If 3 ℓ 75 ml of water are added into the pail, how much more water is needed to make it full?

3. A tank was filled with 2 ℓ 759 ml of water. After another 1 ℓ 948 ml of water were added into the tank, it became half filled with water. What was the capacity of the tank?

4. Two containers containing 4 ℓ 65 ml and 3 ℓ 837 ml of water respectively are poured into a third container containing 2 ℓ 964 ml of water. How much water is there in the third container now?

5. A large pail had 8 ℓ 22 ml of water. Alice used 3 ℓ 477 ml of the water. She then refilled the pail with 4 ℓ 89 ml of water. How much water was there in the pail in the end?

6. Mrs Lai adds 1 ℓ 14 ml of orange syrup and 759 ml of lemon syrup to 11 ℓ 423 ml of water to make a drink. How much drink does she make in all?

7. A container has 451 ml of water. When 1 ℓ 35 ml of water is poured into it, 368 ml of water overflowed. What is the capacity of the container?

8. The table below shows the ingredients used to make a mixed fruit juice. How much mixed fruit juice was made?

INGREDIENTS	AMOUNT
Orange juice	1 ℓ 86 ml
Watermelon juice	1 ℓ 659 ml
Pineapple juice	847 ml
Apple juice	907 ml

9. A jug contained 1 ℓ 118 ml of water. 488 ml of the water was poured into a bowl and the rest was poured into 5 mugs equally. Find the amount of water in each mug.

10. An empty bottle can hold 2 litres of water. If 8 glasses containing 342 ml of water each are poured into the bottle, how much water will spill?

11. Container P can hold 277 ml of water. Container Q can hold six times as much water as container P. How much water can both containers hold in all? Give your answer in litres and millilitres.

12. Pail M has 7 ℓ 20 ml of water. It has 3 ℓ 511 ml of water more than pail N. How much water is there in pails M and N?

Solve each of these problems, showing your working and statements clearly.

13. A bottle when full can hold 1 ℓ 373 ml of water. A pot when full can hold 2 ℓ 768 ml of water more than the bottle. If the pot is holding 2 ℓ 247 ml of water and 2 ℓ 48 ml more water is added to the pot, how much water will overflow?

14. Container A can hold 853 ml of water. Container B can hold eight times as much water as container A. Container C can hold 4 ℓ 838 ml of water less than container B. What is the capacity of container C?

15. A tank had 6 ℓ 10 ml of water. Water began to leak at a rate of 219 ml per minute. At the same time, water was added to the tank at a rate of 166 ml per minute from a tap. Find the amount of water in the tank after 4 minutes.

16. Three empty containers, P, Q and R, have capacitites of 4 ℓ 346 ml, 5 ℓ 110 ml and 3 ℓ 761 ml, respectively. 10 litres of water are poured into P until it is full. The remaining water is then poured into Q until it is full. The rest of the water is poured into R. How much more water can R hold?

17. Pail A contains 771 ml of water. It contains half as much water as pail B and thrice as much water as pail C. Find the total amount of water in pails B and C.

18. 9 cups can hold 296 ml of water each. If each cup is filled with 175 ml of water, how much more water is needed to fill all the cups completely?

19. A container is completely filled with 2 ℓ 970 ml of liquid X, 5 ℓ 128 ml of liquid Y and 1 ℓ 68 ml of liquid Z. If 1 ℓ 492 ml of liquid X, 2 ℓ 337 ml of liquid Y and 474 ml of liquid Z are replaced with water, how much water is needed?

20. Five pails are each filled with water. The first pail is filled with 10 litres of water. The second pail is filled with 1 litre of water less than the first pail, the third pail is filled with 1 litre of water less than the second pail, and so on. Find the total amount of water in the five pails.

21. Three tanks, A, B and C are filled with water. A has thrice as much water as B and B has thrice as much water as C. A has 48 litres of water more than C. Find the total amount of water in the three tanks.

GRAPHS

WORKED EXAMPLE 1

The graph below shows Perry's savings in a certain week.
a. How much did he save on Wednesday?
b. How much more did he save on Thursday than on Tuesday?
c. How much did he save on Friday and Saturday altogether?

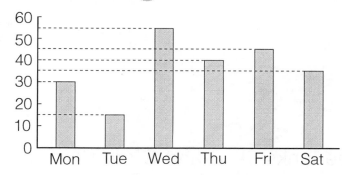

Savings in cents

Days of the week

a. He saved **55¢** on Wednesday.

b. 40 − 15 = 25
   He saved **25¢** more.

c. 45 + 35 = 80
   He saved **80¢** altogether.

Study each graph carefully and then answer the questions that follow.

1. The graph below shows the number of Pat's pets.

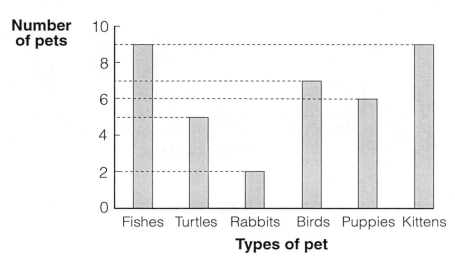

a. How many birds does Pat have?

7

b. How many more fishes than rabbits does she have?

7

c. How many fewer turtles than kittens does she have?

4

2. The graph below shows the number of animals on Mr Keith's farm.

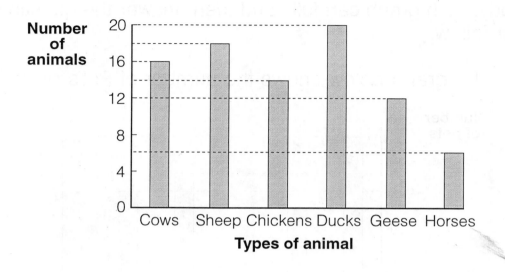

a. How many more ducks than geese are there?

b. How many fewer horses than sheep are there?

c. How many cows and chickens are there?

3. The graph below shows the number of stamps 6 children have.

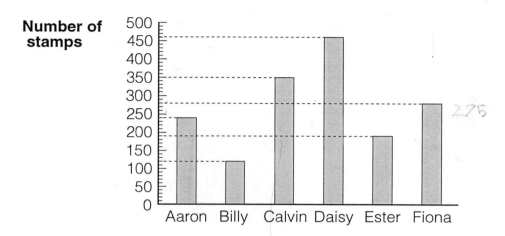

Number of stamps

a. How many more stamps does Daisy have than Fiona?

b. How many fewer stamps does Ester have than Aaron?

c. How many stamps do Billy, Calvin and Fiona have altogether?

4. The graph below shows the amount of money 6 children have.

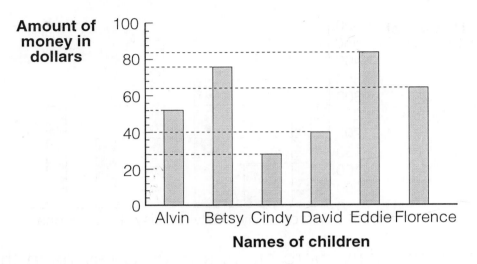

a. How much money do Betsy and Cindy have in all?

b. How much less money does Alvin have than Eddie?

c. How much money do all the children have altogether?

5. The graph below shows the number of shirts Larry sold in a week.

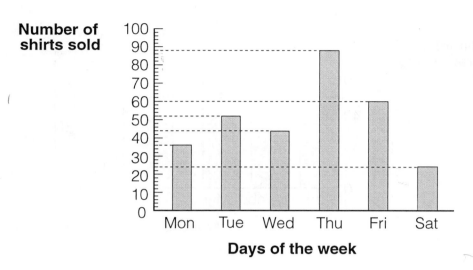

Number of shirts sold

Number of shirts sold (y-axis: 0, 10, 20, 30, 40, 50, 60, 70, 80, 90, 100)

Days: Mon, Tue, Wed, Thu, Fri, Sat

Days of the week

a. How many more shirts did he sell on Friday than on Monday?

b. How many more shirts did he sell on Thursday than on Saturday?

c. How many shirts did he sell from Tuesday to Friday altogether?

6. The graph below shows the number of radio sets Alan sold in different months.

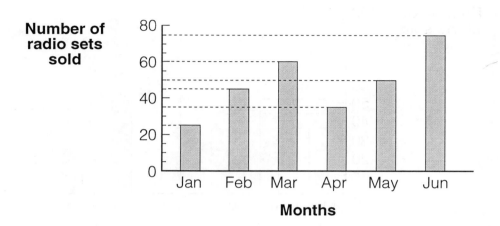

Number of radio sets sold

Months

a. How many fewer radio sets did he sell in January than in March?

b. How many more radio sets did he sell in June than in April?

c. Find the total number of radio sets he sold in the 6 months.

TIME

WORKED EXAMPLE 1

Jack woke up at 11.25 a.m. He jogged for 48 min and cycled for 1 h 6 min before returning home. At what time did he return home?

11:25 a.m.

48 min

1 h 6 min

?

48 min + 1 h 6 min = 1 h 54 min

The total length of time he took to jog and cycle was 1 h 54 min.

11:25 a.m. + 1 h 54 min = 1:19 p.m.

He returned home at **1:19 p.m.**

WORKED EXAMPLE 2

Mark took 2 h 34 min to do his Mathematics homework. He took 27 min more to do his English homework than his Mathematics homework. How long did he take to do both his Mathematics and English homework?

2 h 34 min

Mathematics

27 min } ?

English

2 h 34 min + 27 min = 3 h 1 min

He took 3 h 1 min to do his English homework.

2 h 34 min + 3 h 1 min = 5 h 35 min

He took **5 h 35 min** to do both his Mathematics and English homework.

WORKED EXAMPLE 3

Lionel and James took a total of 6 min 18 s to solve a Mathematics problem. If Lionel took 2 min 20 s less than James, how long did James take?

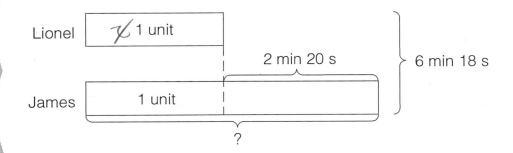

Lionel | 1 unit

2 min 20 s

6 min 18 s

James | 1 unit

?

6 min 18 s – 2 min 20 s = 3 min 58 s

2 units ⟶ 3 min 58 s

1 unit ⟶ 3 min 58 s ÷ 2
= 1 min 59 s

1 min 59 s + 2 min 20 s = 4 min 19 s

James took **4 min 19 s**.

Read and then solve each question carefully. Show your working and statements clearly.

1. A show starts at 6.45 p.m. and ends at 7.50 p.m. How long is the show?

2. Perry's Maths lesson started from 11.40 a.m. and ended at 12.15 p.m. How long was his Maths lesson?

3. A shop is open from 9.30 a.m. to 10 p.m. For how long is it open?

4. A salesgirl works 8 h 40 min a day. If she starts work at 10.30 a.m., at what time does her work end?

5. A show lasting 2 h 14 min ended at 3.03 p.m. At what time did it start?

6. Jenny is 11 years 3 months old. Ali is 2 years 5 months younger than Jenny. How old will Ali be 1 year 6 months later?

7. In a period of 5 years, Mr Mo has worked as a clerk for 1 year 8 months, a salesman for 2 years 5 months and a teacher for the remaining time. For how long has he been a teacher?

8. Xuefang can type 62 words in 1 minute. Lina can type 5 words less than Xuefang in 1 minute. How many words can Lina type in 5 minutes?

9. Meilian took 4 min 15 s to wrap a gift. Huifen took 49 s more than Meilian to wrap the same gift but 23 s less than Aihua. How long did Aihua take to wrap the gift?

10. A man works from 5 p.m. to 11 p.m. each day. If he is paid $3 per hour, how much does he earn each day?

11. Miss Lu earns $35 each day. She spends $26 each day and saves the rest. How much does she save each week?

12. Peiqi and Meihua took a total of 3 weeks 2 days to complete a project. If Peiqi took 1 week 5 days, how much longer did she take than Meihua?

Solve each of these problems, showing your working and statements clearly.

13. Peihua played badminton from 9.12 a.m. to 10.06 a.m. He played badminton again from 4.54 p.m. to 6.11 p.m. For how long did he play badminton in all?

14. Ahmad spent 1 h 28 min to complete his Maths homework and 1 h 35 min to complete his English homework. If he completed all his homework by 6.10 p.m., at what time did he start doing his homework?

15. School functions from 7.35 a.m. to 1.00 p.m. Recess is from 9.50 a.m. to 10.20 a.m. If Mike is in the class for the rest of the day, how long is he in the class?

16. Junxin had to meet his friends at 3.30 p.m. He left his house at 1.55 p.m. and spent 22 min waiting for his bus and 1 h 49 min on the bus. If he met his friends immediately after that, how late was he?

17. Mr Liu has worked in a company for 7 years 9 months. Mr Chen has worked in the same company 4 years 5 months longer than Mr Liu. How long have they worked in the company altogether?

18. The total age of Jack and Peter is 25 years 2 months. If Peter is 12 years 11 months old, how old was Jack 4 years 7 months ago?

19. 5 years 9 months ago, John was 7 years 8 months old. How old will he be 4 years 3 months later?

20. For every half hour parking in a car park, a car owner has to pay $2 parking fee. If he parks his car there for 4 hours, how much parking fee must he pay?

21. Mr Mo is paid $6 for every hour that he works. If he works 8 hours each day and 6 days each week, how much does he earn in 3 weeks?

22. There are 58 machines in a factory. Each machine can make 9 toys in each hour. If they operate from 8.00 a.m. to 5.00 p.m. from Monday to Friday, how many toys can the factory make each week?

23. A tour to China is twice as long as a tour to Thailand. If both tours last 5 weeks 1 day altogether, how long is the tour to China?

24. The total age of Janet and Pam is 21 years 1 month old. If Janet is 7 months older than Pam, how old is Pam?

TOPICAL PROBLEMS 9

AREA AND PERIMETER

WORKED EXAMPLE 1

The figure shows a rectangle. Find its area and perimeter.

14 m

9 m

Area of rectangle = Length × Breadth

14 × 9 = 126

The area of the rectangle is **126 m²**.

Perimeter of rectangle = Length + Length + Breadth + Breadth

14 + 14 + 9 + 9 = 46

The perimeter of the rectangle is **46 m**.

The figure shows a rectangular farm. How much does it cost to fence it at $6 per metre?

65 m

43 m

Perimeter of rectangle = Length + Length + Breadth + Breadth

65 + 65 + 43 + 43 = 216

The perimeter of the farm is 216 m.

$216 \times 6 = 1\ 296$

It costs **$1 296** to fence it at $6 per metre.

The figure shows the floor of a rectangular room. How much does it cost to carpet it at $8 per square metre?

8 m

6 m

Area of rectangle = Length × Breadth

$8 \times 6 = 48$

The area of the floor is 48 m².

$48 \times 8 = 384$

It costs **$384** to carpet it at $8 per square metre.

Read and then solve each question carefully. Show your working and statements clearly.

1. The figure shows a rectangular cabbage farm. Find its area and perimeter.

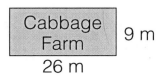

2. A rectangular cardboard is 17 cm long and 10 cm wide. What is its area and perimeter?

3. A square is 8 cm long. Find its area and perimeter.

4. The figure shows a rectangular bookmark. Find its area and perimeter.

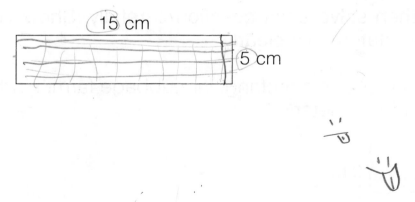

15 cm

5 cm

5. The figure shows a rectangular piece of land. Find its area and perimeter.

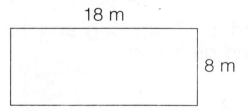

18 m

8 m

6. A rectangular field was 176 m long and 66 m wide. Michael ran around it thrice. Find the distance he ran.

Challenging Problems

Solve each of these problems, showing your working and statements clearly.

7. A rectangular piece of land is twice as long as it is wide. If it is 27 m wide, find its perimeter.

8. A rectangular painting is thrice as long as it is wide. If it is 54 cm long, find its area.

9. A piece of wire is 36 cm long. It is bent to form a square. What is its area?

10. Find the perimeter of the figure shown.

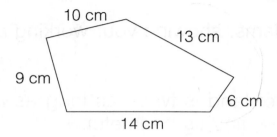

11. In the figure shown, find its perimeter.

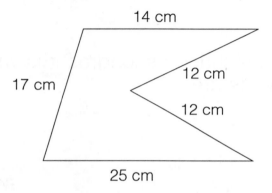

12. What is the perimeter of the figure shown?

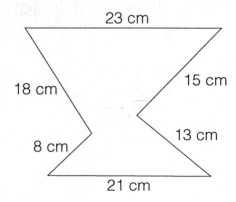

13. A rectangular picture is 14 cm long and 4 cm wide. Another rectangular picture is as long as the first picture but twice as wide. What is the area of the second picture?

14. The diagram shows two rectangular pictures. How much larger is the area of picture A than that of picture B?

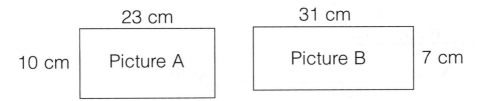

15. The diagram below shows a picture mounted on a cardboard. What is the area of the cardboard not covered by the picture?

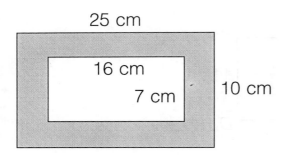

16. The diagram shows a piece of cloth cut into 4 equal squares. What is the area of each square?

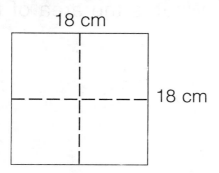

18 cm

18 cm

17. The figure ABCDE has a perimeter of 42 cm. What is the length of ED?

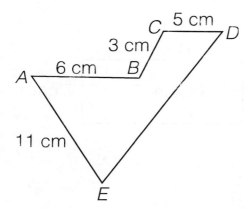

18. The figure ABCDE has a perimeter of 55 cm. If AB = AE, what is the length of AB?

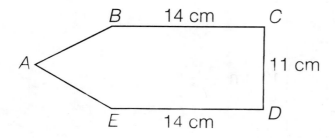

19. The figure ABCDEF has a perimeter of 52 cm. If AB is shorter than ED by 8 cm, what is the length of AB?

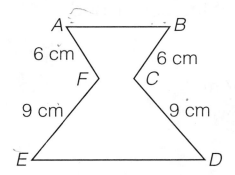

20. The figure ABCDE has a perimeter of 57 cm. If AB = BC and AE = CD, find the length of ED.

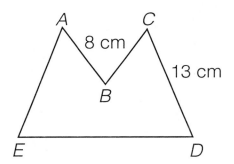

21. What is the perimeter of the figure shown?

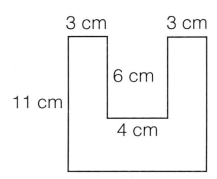

22. The figure shows a rectangular garden. A gardener wants to build a 1-metre flower bed around its perimeter. Find the area of the flower bed.

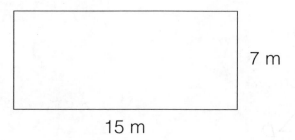

7 m

15 m

23. The figure shown is made up of two rectangles. Find its area.

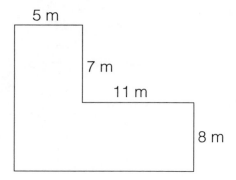

5 m

7 m

11 m

8 m

24. The figure shown is made up of a square and a rectangle. What is its area?

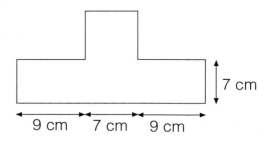

7 cm

9 cm   7 cm   9 cm

REVISION PROBLEMS 2

Read and then answer each question carefully. Show your working and statements clearly.

1. Mrs Deng bought three soft toys for $57·50, $21·90 and $17·60 respectively. If she paid the cashier $100, how much change did she get?

2. 3 tables are sold at $165 each. If the same amount of money can buy 5 chairs, how much does each chair cost?

3. Mr Lin bought 7 notebooks at $3 each and 4 writing pads at $2 each. How much money did he spend altogether?

4. Mr Chen's monthly income is $1 245. If he spends $798 each month, how much money can he save in half a year?

5. A container with a capacity of 7 ℓ 45 ml has 4 ℓ 865 ml of water. If 6 ℓ 70 ml of water are added to the container, how much water will overflow?

6. A bottle contains 3 litres of orange juice. 7 glasses of 235 ml of orange juice are poured from the bottle. How many litres and millilitres of orange juice are left in the bottle?

7. 1 ℓ of petrol costs $1. Mr Fu buys 25 ℓ of petrol. If he pays with 3 $10 notes, how much change will he get?

8. Amy spent 2 h 40 min to revise her Mathematics homework. If she finished her revision at 6.10 p.m., at what time did she start her revision?

9. Three shows last 1 h 57 min, 2 h 18 min and 1 h 45 min respectively. If Norman watches all three shows continuously, how long will he take?

10. Sam and Johnny have a total age of 27 years 5 months. If Sam is 12 years 4 months old, how much younger is he than Johnny?

11. A rectangular piece of land is 76 m long and 10 m wide. If it has a pond with an area of 399 m² in it and the rest of it is covered with grass, what area of the land is covered with grass?

12. A rectangular running track measured 214 m by 111 m. John ran round it thrice. What was the total distance covered by John?

13. Mary has a rectangular drawing which measures 43 cm by 29 cm. She wants to stick a piece of ribbon all around the edge of the drawing. If her ribbon measures 95 cm long, how much more ribbon does she need?

14. Jack has a piece of wire 120 cm long. He bent it to form a rectangle 34 cm long. What is the width of the rectangle formed?

15. The graph below shows the number of coloured balloons May has.

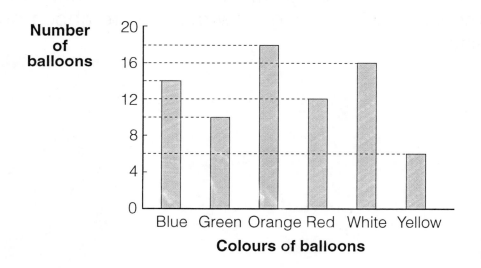

Number of balloons

Colours of balloons

a. How many more orange balloons than yellow balloons does May have?

b. How many fewer red balloons than white balloons are there?

c. How many balloons are there altogether?

Solve each of these problems, showing your working and statements clearly.

16. Two waiters, Jack and Moses, work in the same cafe. Jack is paid $168 for every working week while Moses is paid $640 monthly. How much less will Moses be paid than Jack in a month with 28 working days?

17. Each T-shirt costs $18. Each blouse costs $5 more than each T-shirt. Find the total cost of 7 T-shirts and 6 blouses.

18. A sum of $144 is divided among 3 boys and 2 girls. Each boy gets twice as much as each girl. How much money do the 2 girls get altogether?

19. An empty tank has a hole at its base where water can flow out at a rate of 74 ml per minute. Two taps are turned on to add water into the tank at rates of 220 ml and 415 ml per minute respectively. How much water is there in the tank after 5 minutes?

20. Water is poured into 5 empty containers so that the first container has 2 litres of water less than the second container, the second container has 2 litres of water less than the third container, and so on. If the first container has 16 litres of water, how many litres of water are there in the 5 containers?

21. Three tanks are each half filled with water. The amounts of water in the tanks are 67 litres, 94 litres and 135 litres respectively. What is the total capacity of the three tanks?

22. A shop was open from 10.20 a.m. to 7.15 p.m. There was a power failure from 11.45 a.m. to 12.30 p.m. and the lights were out. For how long were the lights on?

23. A worker was paid $4 hourly before 9 p.m. and $6 hourly after 9 p.m. If he worked from 5 p.m. to 11 p.m. yesterday, how much money was he paid?

24. A photocopier took 2 minutes to photocopy 10 sheets of paper. Mr Li started photocopying 500 sheets of paper at 4.55 p.m. At what time did he finish photocopying?

25. In the diagram shown, what is the area of the figure?

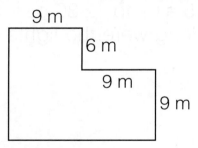

9 m
6 m
9 m
9 m

26. The figure shown has a perimeter of 84 cm.
If $AB = BC$, find the length of AB.

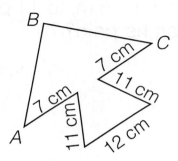

27. The figure shown has a perimeter of 52 cm. If AB is shorter than CD by 2 cm, find the length of AB.

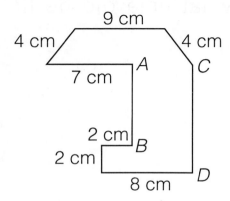

Practice Problems

Read and then answer each question carefully. Show your working and statements clearly.

1. Aaron has 3 411 stamps. He has 793 more stamps than Sam and 1 266 fewer stamps than John. How many stamps do Sam and John have altogether?

2. Mr Chen's monthly income is $2 400. He spent $1 732 in May and $1 569 in June. How much money did he save in these two months?

3. 483 paper clips were shared equally among 7 pupils. If one of them lost 13 paper clips, how many paper clips had he left?

4. There were a dozen eggs in each pack. Mrs Ma bought 6 packs and broke 3 eggs. How many eggs had she left?

5. Mother bought 2 packets of 136 sweets each. She shared them equally among 8 children. How many sweets did each child get?

6. Rick has thrice as many shells as Jill. If they have 92 shells altogether, how many shells does Rick have?

7. Annie and Tracy took part in a 10-km run. After some time, Annie was 4 km 567 m away from the finishing line while Tracy was 6 km 98 m away from the starting point. What was the total distance they had run?

8. An empty container weighing 433 g, contains 1 kg 28 g of mint sweets and 2 kg 739 g of strawberry sweets. Find the total weight of the bottle of sweets.

9. $72 was shared among 9 children. If one of the children spent $5·90, how much money did he have left?

10. Miss Pan saved $233 each month. After saving up for 9 months, she spent $968. How much money had she left?

11. Bottle X contains five times as much fruit juice as bottle Y. If there are 936 ml of fruit juice in both bottles, how much more fruit juice is there in bottle X than bottle Y?

12. Claire took 6 min 17 s to solve a jigsaw puzzle. Lisa took 1 min 22 s less than Claire. How long did both of them take altogether?

13. A rectangular farm is 78 m long and 63 m wide. If it costs $6 to fence each metre of the farm, how much will it cost to fence the whole farm?

14. A rectangular room is 4 m long and half as wide as it is long. How much will it cost to tile the whole room at $247 per square metre?

15. The graph below shows the number of letters which Pat typed in a certain week.

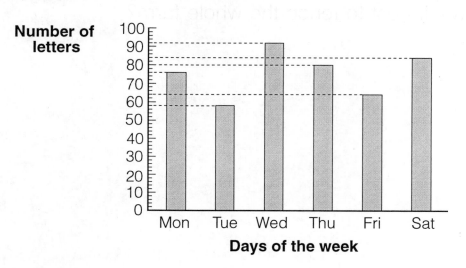

Number of letters

Days of the week

a. How many more letters did she type on Wednesday than on Friday?

b. How many fewer letters did she type on Tuesday than on Saturday?

c. How many letters did she type in the week altogether?

Solve each of these problems, showing your working and statements clearly.

16. Danny and Paul had the same number of marbles. After Danny gave 36 marbles to Paul, he had half as many marbles as Paul. How many marbles did they have altogether?

17. Rose had 86 more pencils than pens. After she gave away 17 pencils, she had four times as many pencils as pens. How many pencils and pens had she left?

18. William has 77 more picture cards than Ron. Both of them have 213 picture cards altogether. If William gives 16 picture cards to Ron, how many more picture cards will William have than Ron?

19. Richard has 176 more bookmarks than Adrian. Daniel has 99 fewer bookmarks than Richard. The three boys have 415 bookmarks in all. How many bookmarks does Adrian have?

20. String M was 5 m 18 cm longer than string N. After part of string M was cut, it was 2 m 44 cm shorter than string N. Find the length of string M that was cut away.

21. There are three bags of soil, A, B and C. A is six times as heavy as B and twice as heavy as C. A and C have a total weight of 945 g. How much lighter is B than C?

22. Rachel and Cindy have $126 altogether. If Rachel gives $15 to Cindy, Cindy will have twice as much money as Rachel. How much money does Cindy have?

23. Each jacket costs $250. Each shirt costs $191 less than each jacket. How much do 3 jackets and 7 shirts cost in all?

24. A tank had 261 litres of water. The water was then pumped out through two pipes at rates of 4 litres per minute and 5 litres per minute respectively. How long did it take to empty the tank?

25. A shop is open from 11 a.m. to 9 p.m. from Mondays to Fridays, and from 10 a.m. to 10 p.m. on Saturdays and Sundays. For how many hours is it open each week?

26. A rectangle has a length of 17 cm and a perimeter of 50 cm. What is its area?

27. In the diagram shown, both rectangles have the same perimeter. What is the length of rectangle *B*?

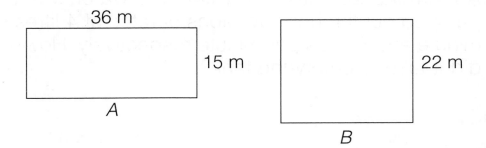

ANSWERS

TOPICAL PROBLEMS 1

Practice Problems

1. 443	2. 8 429	3. 2 552
4. 220	5. 1 244	6. 1 151
7. 49	8. 23	9. 7 652
10. 2 018	11. 3 581	12. 4 865

Challenging Problems

13. 2 382	14. 368	15. 4 103
16. 145	17. 1 516	18. 88
19. 17	20. 13	21. 48
22. 97	23. 7	24. 180

TOPICAL PROBLEMS 2

Practice Problems

1. 95	2. 615	3. 24
4. 34	5. 67	6. 120
7. 132	8. 63	9. 156
10. 253	11. 78	12. 170

Challenging Problems

13. 41	14. 41	15. 24
16. 1 199	17. 688	18. 112
19. 58	20. 28	21. 56
22. 256	23. 63	24. 42

TOPICAL PROBLEMS 3

Practice Problems

1. 12 m 25 cm	2. 88 m
3. 1 m 80 cm	4. 1 m 60 cm
5. 14 cm	6. 4 m 65 cm
7. 10 m 2 cm	8. 7 km 188 m
9. 8 m 40 cm	10. 684 cm
11. 6 km 632 m	

Challenging Problems

12. 16 m 79 cm	13. 7 m 4 cm
14. 1 m 92 cm	15. 1 m 69 cm
16. 318 cm	17. 172 cm
18. 1 km 223 m	19. 186 cm
20. 84 cm	

TOPICAL PROBLEMS 4

Practice Problems

1. 9 kg 671 g	2. 53 kg 425 g
3. 265 g	4. 528 g
5. 97 g	6. 70 g
7. 123 kg 745 g	8. 4 kg 590 g
9. 1 450 g	10. 2 kg 932 g
11. 2 kg 970 g	12. 1 644 g

Challenging Problems

13. 52 kg	14. 199 g	15. 700 g
16. 325 g	17. 864 g	18. 180 kg
19. 894 g	20. 163 g	21. $4

REVISION PROBLEMS 1

Practice Problems

1. 2 162	2. 2 868
3. 2 372	4. 713
5. 63	6. 165
7. 79	8. 129
9. 1 491	10. 2 848
11. 63	12. 1 m 57 cm
13. 5 km 342 m	14. $5
15. 54 g	16. $91
17. 1 kg 853 g	

Challenging Problems

18. 29	19. 72
20. 89	21. 48
22. 115	23. 57
24. 625 m	25. 600 m
26. 2 m 9 cm	27. 5 kg 500 g
28. 560 g	29. 410 g

TOPICAL PROBLEMS 5

Practice Problems

1. $62·00	2. $96·60	3. $35·10
4. $153·70	5. $15·30	6. $594
7. $0·80	8. $16	9. $19·15
10. $3	11. $6	12. $17·25

Challenging Problems

13. $19·40
14. $55
15. $2·85
16. $7·20
17. $200
18. $15
19. $4·85
20. $20
21. 48
22. 2
23. $3 459

TOPICAL PROBLEMS 6

Practice Problems

1. 7 ℓ 341 ml
2. 5 ℓ 925 ml
3. 9 ℓ 414 ml
4. 10 ℓ 866 ml
5. 8 ℓ 634 ml
6. 13 ℓ 196 ml
7. 1 ℓ 118 ml
8. 4 ℓ 499 ml
9. 126 ml
10. 736 ml
11. 1 ℓ 939 ml
12. 10 ℓ 529 ml

Challenging Problems

13. 154 ml
14. 1 ℓ 986 ml
15. 5 ℓ 798 ml
16. 3 ℓ 217 ml
17. 1 ℓ 799 ml
18. 1 089 ml
19. 4 ℓ 303 ml
20. 40 litres
21. 78 litres

TOPICAL PROBLEMS 7

Practice Problems

1. (a) 7   (b) 7   (c) 4
2. (a) 8   (b) 12   (c) 30
3. (a) 180   (b) 50   (c) 750
4. (a) $104   (b) $32   (c) $344
5. (a) 24   (b) 64   (c) 244
6. (a) 35   (b) 40   (c) 290

TOPICAL PROBLEMS 8

Practice Problems

1. 1 h 5 min
2. 35 min
3. 12 h 30 min
4. 7.10 p.m.
5. 12.49 p.m.
6. 10 years 4 months
7. 11 months
8. 285
9. 5 min 27 s
10. $18
11. $63
12. 1 day

Challenging Problems

13. 2 h 11 min
14. 3.07 p.m.
15. 4 h 55 min
16. 36 min
17. 19 years 11 months
18. 7 years 8 months
19. 17 years 8 months
20. $16
21. $864
22. 23 490
23. 3 weeks 3 days
24. 10 years 4 months

TOPICAL PROBLEMS 9

Practice Problems

1. 234 m², 70 m
2. 170 cm², 54 cm
3. 64 cm², 32 cm
4. 75 cm², 40 cm
5. 144 m², 52 m
6. 1 452 m
7. 162 m
8. 972 cm²
9. 81 cm²
10. 52 cm
11. 80 cm
12. 98 cm

Challenging Problems

13. 112 cm²
14. 13 cm²
15. 138 cm²
16. 81 cm²
17. 17 cm
18. 8 cm
19. 7 cm
20. 15 cm
21. 54 cm
22. 48 m²
23. 163 cm²
24. 224 cm²

REVISIONS PROBLEMS 2

Practice Problems

1. $3·00
2. $99
3. $29
4. $2 682
5. 3 ℓ 890 ml
6. 1 ℓ 355 ml
7. $5
8. 3.30 p.m.
9. 6 hours
10. 2 years 9 months
11. 361 m²
12. 1 950 m
13. 49 m
14. 26 cm
15. (a) 12   (b) 4   (c) 76

Challenging Problems

16. $32
17. $264

18. $36
19. 2 805 ml
20. 110 litres
21. 592 litres
22. 8 h 10 min
23. $28
24. 5.45 p.m.
25. 216 m²
26. 18 cm
27. 7 cm

REVISION PROBLEMS 3

Practice Problems

1. 7 295
2. $1 499
3. 56
4. 69
5. 34
6. 69

7. 11 km 531 m
8. 4 kg 200 g
9. $2·10
10. $1 129
11. 624 ml
12. 11 min 12 s
13. $1 692
14. $1 976
15. (a) 28   (b) 26   (c) 454

Challenging Problems

16. 216
17. 115
18. 45
19. 54
20. 7 m 62 cm
21. 210 g
22. $69
23. $1 163
24. 29 minutes
25. 74 hours
26. 136 cm²
27. 29 m